Teaching and learning in the twenty-first century

Chris Husbands

Teaching and learning in the twenty-first century

What is an 'institute of education' for?

Professor Chris Husbands

Based on an Inaugural Directorial Lecture delivered at the Institute of Education, University of London, on 28 November 2011

Institute of Education, University of London

IOE
LONDON

**Leading education
and social research**
Institute of Education
University of London

First published in 2012 by the Institute of Education, University of London,
20 Bedford Way, London WC1H 0AL
www.ioe.ac.uk/publications

British Library Cataloguing in Publication Data:
A catalogue record for this publication is available from the British Library

ISBN 978 0 85473 918 9

The opinions expressed in this publication are those of
the author and do not necessarily reflect the views of
the Institute of Education, University of London.

The author and publisher gratefully acknowledge the permission
granted to reproduce the copyright material in this book.

Photo of a 19th century classroom reprinted with
permission of Woodhouse Grove School.

Figure 2 reprinted with permission from Princeton University Press.

Every effort has been made to trace copyright holders and to
obtain their permission for the use of copyright material. The
publisher apologises for any errors or omissions in the above list
and would be grateful if notified of any corrections that should
be incorporated in future reprints or editions of this book.

Typeset by Quadrant Infotech (India) Pvt Ltd
Printed by ImageData Group

Biography

Professor Chris Husbands is Director of the Institute of Education, University of London. He read history and completed a doctorate at the University of Cambridge before beginning his career teaching in secondary schools. He was a teacher and senior manager in urban comprehensive schools before moving into higher education; he was formerly Director of the Institute of Education at Warwick University and Dean of Education and Lifelong Learning at the University of East Anglia. He is currently a Board Member at the Training and Development Agency for Schools, and a member of the advisory Learning Panel at the National Trust. He has also served as a Board member at two examining groups – Edexcel and the Assessment and Qualifications Alliance. He has worked as a consultant or adviser to local authorities, OFSTED, the DfE, the Qualifications and Curriculum Authority and the National College for Leadership in Schools and Children's Services; internationally he has worked with the Ministry of Higher Education in Dubai, the Ministry of Education in Egypt and with Microsoft Education in Taiwan. Professor Husbands has research interests in teacher education and education policy. He was director of the National Evaluation of Children's Trusts, which explored the relationships between teachers and other professionals in supporting children's well-being (2004–8), led a review of children's outcomes in high performing education systems for the Department for Education (2008–9), and the evaluation of the national development programme for directors of children's services. He led the UK component of the International Alliance of Leading Education Institute's report on *Transforming teacher education* (2008) and on education and climate change (2009). He has written widely on aspects of education policy and on curriculum and teacher development, and retains an interest in the teaching and learning of history.

Teaching and learning in the twenty-first century: what is an 'institute of education' for?

Beginnings...the Institute of Education and London

November 2011. Monday morning, 8.30 a.m. Pupils arrive at their school in London. The weekend is over. The school week begins. What moulds the way, in 2011, in which these young people think, work and learn? What frames the way their teachers plan and teach? How do classrooms respond to the huge forces shaping the world in which these young people live? What does an institute of education have to say to them?

The Institute of Education (IOE) was established on 6 October 1902 as the London Day Training College. As Richard Aldrich's history of the Institute explains, its origins lay in the transformation of education in London which followed the 1870 Education Act and the introduction of compulsory elementary education. The London School Board faced considerable challenges: with 2,000 schools educating a million children, most of its 20,000 teachers were untrained or inadequately trained.[1] The foundation of the College depended on drawing together the School Board, London County Council, the Board of Education and the University of London, a task in which Sidney Webb – Fabian socialist, economist and social reformer – was instrumental. The first appointment and the first principal of the College was John Adams, recruited from Glasgow as the University of London's first professor of the Theory, History and Practice of Education. Addressing the Institute's first 58 students at the College's opening, Adams set out his priorities for the education of teachers:

The training of the teacher consists primarily in...acquiring...knowledge of child-nature and the materials upon which that nature works...The science of education must begin and end with the child.[2]

Webb's vision was of a postgraduate university in the heart of London, which would provide 'an intellectual pre-eminence to complement and reinforce the city's imperial, financial, and commercial pre-eminence.'[3] Webb was clear that:

> *A university is, or ought to be, much more than a mere place for teaching. Its most important function...is the advancement of every branch of learning...In the whole range of the physical and biological sciences, in the newer fields of anthropology, archaeology, philology, pedagogy and experimental psychology, in the wide vistas opening out for applied science and the highest technology, in the constantly changing spheres of industrial and commercial relations, administration and political organisations, we may predict with confidence that a richly organised and adequately endowed London University will take a foremost part in the advancement of learning.*[4]

I begin at the foundation of the Institute for several reasons. First, because, like the other university establishments of the later nineteenth century,[5] the Institute was enmeshed in the civic structures of the period, part of wider efforts to mobilise local resources to enable urban, industrial society to socialise its population: the Institute was of its time.[6] Second, I want to highlight a tension in the way the founders of the London Day Training College – which formally became the Institute in 1932[7] – saw the role of the organisation: on the one hand it focused on the children, teachers and schools of London, on the other, it was part of an expansive vision of a globally ambitious postgraduate university whose role was to advance learning. This tension between the local and the global – sometimes creative, sometimes less so – shaped the way the Institute developed and gave it a distinctive flavour. I also begin in this way to make the important point that while the Institute has in many ways achieved the aspirations of Sidney Webb, it has also gone beyond them and has established itself not 'merely' as a centre for postgraduate training and research in education but as a major centre for research and inquiry in social science and social policy more generally. The Institute in 2011 draws together leading scholarship in education, but also in sociology, social policy, public economics and quantitative social science – it is a national and international research powerhouse in its own right, ranked among the top three or four social science research institutions in the United Kingdom.[8]

An inaugural directorial lecture is something of a novelty: there are obvious expectations about putting down markers not just of my own thinking but also of the development of the institution, and to do that for a diverse audience of academics, policy-makers and practitioners. I shall try to do this by revisiting some of the questions implicitly posed by John Adams and Sidney Webb more than a century ago and to raise some questions about the nature, role and function of an 'institute of education' – this Institute of Education – at the beginning of the twenty-first century. I shall do so by exploring the pressures and changes in the education system nationally and globally. I shall betray my own concerns, and – as I hope is acceptable in an inaugural lecture – will range widely over the related landscape of schooling, teaching and learning. As such, I shall omit much in thinking about the role and nature of the Institute and the world in which it operates, and to this I can only respond that in front of so distinguished an audience, I shall try to talk about what I know. My comments, however, about teaching and learning, and about teachers and schools are, I hope, more widely generalisable about social science and social policy research and practice.

Continuities and disruptions...London and beyond

There have been some remarkable continuities in the educational landscape over the Institute's first hundred years, all of them fundamental to schooling. Some of these continuities – in the typical layout of learning spaces, nature of classroom practice, structuring of the curriculum and overall form of schools – have been in place for centuries, and well beyond London. They seem essentially impervious to wider disruptions and upheavals – from Henry of Germany, lecturing in Bologna in the mid-fourteenth century,[9] through the classrooms of late nineteenth century London,[10] to the schools of today (Figure 1). In all, we see familiar features: a teacher at the front of the room, addressing the learners, learners arranged in rows before the teacher, learning structured in blocks of time built around a demarcated curriculum. These are characteristics, instantly recognisable, of classrooms the world over. The regular MORI survey for the Campaign for Learning asks secondary pupils to report the classroom activities in which they engage most often. The 2008 survey – like those of 2000, 2002, 2004 and 2006 – found that the most common activities were listening to the teacher and copying from a board, the very activities which have characterised classrooms over a long period of time.[11]

Figure 1: The classroom: 1340–2011

There are, though, continuities that are more closely and immediately linked to the rationale for and core work of this Institute of Education – that is, the challenges of recruiting, retaining, developing and deploying teachers in a hugely complex global city, and of equipping them with the knowledge and skills they need not only to perform their roles successfully, but also to understand and take responsibility for them. The task that the London Day Training College was established to fulfil is as necessary and formidable as ever, arguably more so. The built-up area of London now includes about 4,000 schools and approximately 80,000 teachers, as well as something over 40 universities. The logistical and intellectual challenges of meeting their needs remain daunting, as Kathryn Riley reminded us in her own inaugural lecture.[12]

A story of stability, however, will not do for us: it is not enough to argue that the Institute today faces the same questions and challenges as the Institute of the later nineteenth century, that urban education is a constant challenge which requires continued application. Some discontinuities are obvious; some less so. London has been transformed in so many ways: physically transformed by two world wars and post-war development; economically transformed by the decline of manufacturing and shipping and the extra-ordinary rise of finance and the service economy, so that it is now, as Giles Fraser put it, 'the boiler room of global capitalism';[13] demographically transformed by patterns of migration and movement;[14] socially transformed by the construction and subsequent remodellings of the welfare state so that disparities in wealth narrowed in the mid-twentieth century and are now widening again;[15] and, of course, educationally transformed, not least through the establishment of universal education, to the age of 14 in 1918, 15 in 1944, 16 in 1973 and, by 2015, 18,[16] as well as the enormous growth of higher education. There are other equally significant transformations. Digital technologies, on-line resources and social networking are changing the way people interact inside and outside formal institutions: the audience at this lecture will be checking their iPhones, iPads and Blackberries even as they (perhaps pretend to) listen to it. Environmental challenges increasingly shape the way we think about the world in which we live. These wider transformative forces have made London a complex world city in an inter-connected world, and underpin the drivers that are reshaping schooling and education reform.

More than ever, the education policy context in which the IOE operates is globalised. Increasingly, educational policy-makers and educational practitioners look across the world for their points of comparison, and policy interventions echo round the globe. More than that, though, a striking feature of education debate has been the extent to which it has, like so many other aspects of social policy and practice, been simultaneously globalised and localised – globalised as international policy borrowing becomes routine, and localised as that exchange is customised to local circumstance: charter schools in the United States[17] become academy and free schools in England;[18] *Teach for America*, a transformational teacher education programme in the United States is exported to England as *Teach First*, to Australia as *Teach for Australia* and now developed as *Teach for All* in countries as diverse as Lebanon, Spain, India and Chile.[19] University Technical Colleges developed to provide vocational training for 14–19 year olds in England mirror the *meister* schools established in South Korea.[20] This trend both reflects and reinforces the growing political rhetoric around the importance of education to the economic prospects of nation states, and therein the growing profile and significance of education within political debate and policy programmes. 'Governments around the world', as Ben Levin points out, 'continue to be intensively involved in changing their education systems.'[21] Reform efforts have been only moderately tempered by what has been described as the most severe financial crisis in modern history[22] and the consequent squeeze on government spending.[23]

Contexts: teaching and learning in the twenty-first century

These changes in the parameters of education debate and the current scale and speed of education reform are significant in themselves, but they are linked to what I want to identify as three major underlying challenges for education systems today. They each call for responses from practice, policy and research and, I will argue, a different relationship between them. These challenges are:

- the challenge of *system performance* in order to better respond to the social and economic context of educational provision in a global context;
- the challenge of *school organisation* in order to optimise the organisation of schools as regards school improvement; and
- the challenge of *improving teaching* in order to achieve a step-change in the way teachers work.

The social and economic context of educational provision: promise and performance

It has been frequently observed that the schooling structures of the later nineteenth century reflected the demands of the industrial economy – the need to provide basic education for the mass of the population before their entry to a labour market dominated by low-skill, routine jobs.[24] It is similarly often observed that the contemporary labour markets of western economies appear to be changing fundamentally once again. According to Autor, Levy and Murnane, the later twentieth century saw a dramatic acceleration in the transition from a labour market comprising jobs substantially requiring routine skills to one demanding complex cognitive and expert-thinking skills (Figure 2).[25] The perceived need of the resulting 'knowledge economy' for more highly-skilled workers has redoubled concerns about the fitness for purpose of conventional educational structures and the quality of schools and schooling, which are strongly reflected in debates about the performance of education systems over time, about comparative system performance and about the current structure and focus of schooling. Broadly speaking, standards of performance in schools in England in terms of the scale and level of pupil attainment have improved markedly. For example, the proportion of young people leaving school with a 'matriculation' level qualification of at least five GCSE grades at C or better has risen from 9 per cent in 1959 to 58 per cent in 2011.[26] Measured performance in reading and mathematics at the end of primary school has also risen. Now, however, the focus is on the comparative performance of education systems drawing on programmes such as PISA (Programme for International Student Assessment), which tests a national sample of 15-year-olds across OECD member countries every three years in literacy, mathematics and science. In a lucid account of the operation of international assessment in education, my colleague Tina Isaacs quotes Hopmann and Brinek, that 'every time a new PISA wave rolls in, or an additional analysis appears, newspapers fill column after column and the public demands answers to failings in the country's school system'.[27] In 2010, England's PISA performance across most indicators was close to the OECD mean,[28] and the overall performance was described by Andreas Schleicher, co-ordinator of PISA, as 'stagnant at best'; while performance in England has plateaued since 2007, the performance of other countries, including Poland and Norway, has continued to improve.

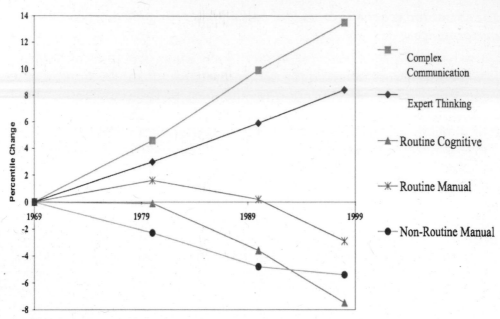

Figure 2: US job skill demand 1969–99 (From Levy, Frank; The New Division of Labour. © 2004 by Russell Sage Foundation. Published by Princeton University Press. Reprinted by permission of Princeton University Press.)

There is a further issue for the English system. As Alma Harris pointed out in her professorial lecture here in 2009,[29] although general levels of attainment have improved over time, the gap between more affluent peers and the majority of children from low-income families has increased. This is a problem in absolute and relative terms. In addition to assessing how well pupils can apply what they have learnt in school to problems, PISA measures consistency of performance across schools and the significance of factors such as socio-economic background on pupil performance. England is notable in its PISA results for having a proportion of pupils whose performance is among the best in the world coupled with a long tail of poorly performing young people. The attainment gap in England remains among the widest of the OECD member countries, while PISA has driven the important positive shift in perception that equity in educational outcomes does not need to be secured at the expense of quality.

The relative performance of England in international assessments has been an important point of reference for recent governments in the UK, but particularly so for the current Coalition, which has looked closely at the education systems of the best performing countries. In the 'glocalised' process of policy borrowing which I outlined earlier, however, the influences on its policy development have been more eclectic and selective. Most notable has been the government's headlining of school and teacher autonomy as the defining features of the best performing systems – and I will say more about that in a moment. However, the degree of central direction that has emerged alongside, with a view to raising standards, narrowing the attainment gap and supporting opportunities for all, is striking. Amid this steerage of schools, substantial debate focuses on the curriculum and the adequacy of what is taught. Debates about the curriculum are deeply embedded, not least because of the intense challenges in assessing what young people will need to know, understand and be able to do over the course of working and adult lives, which we know are being rapidly changed.[30] The debate over the recently designated 'English Baccalaureate' and related performance measures is a good case in point. For its proponents, the English Baccalaureate – based on GCSE success in English, Mathematics, Science, a language and History or Geography – is a mechanism for ensuring that all young people have access to an academic core which is likely to give them access to admission to the best universities and the best employers, and this core is something which is relatively stable and timeless. For its critics, it is simply too narrow and inflexible, reflecting a small range of subjects excluding the arts.[31] Bob Schwartz argues in his report on curriculum issues in American schools, *Pathways to Prosperity*, that:

> *a focus on [university] readiness alone does not equip young people with all of the skills and abilities they will need in the workplace, or to successfully complete the transition from adolescence to adulthood... [We should not] make the mistake of mandating a narrow common curriculum for all.*[32]

There *is* a compelling issue about the curriculum, about what to teach and how to assess it. Practices – and performance measures – need to support high standards for all, not least in literacy, numeracy and core knowledge; I am not complacent about that. But if literacy and numeracy are critical,[33] they are not sufficient;[34] knowledge and its organisation matters, but so does preparation for adulthood. Performance measures need also to support a curriculum that engages all young people and is relevant to them and their future. Ultimately, of course, as Lorna Unwin, David Guile and Laura James have argued, in a knowledge-based economy we need a more developed dialogue between employers and practitioners at all levels of education than has previously been the case.[35]

The organisation of schools and schooling: structures and improvement

The second challenge emerges from questions about the organisation of schools, schooling and other education institutions. The OECD *Schooling for Tomorrow* project was influential in mapping scenarios for schooling in 2020.[36] Based on an analysis of the social, economic and technological change drivers, the project developed six different 'ideal type' scenarios (Figure 3). Two of their scenarios were based on versions of current organisation, anticipating either tighter bureaucratic regulation of schools or the consequences of increased marketisation within current frameworks; two were based on 're-schooling' models envisaging schools developing as either social centres for their communities or as learning hubs; while two others anticipated a move to 'de-schooling' models based on either technologically enabled 'learning networks' replacing some of the functions of schooling, or the development of a full-blown market in learning.

At system level at least we are essentially seeing an evolution of existing provision rather than more radical change in line with the most disruptive scenarios I have just listed – though the pace of change feels marked enough to most of us. In England, that evolution has been in the direction of greater school autonomy, liberalising the supply of education, and removing state agencies and the regulatory frameworks associated with them.[37] The scale of change has perhaps been faster in London than anywhere else in the country. London has always had a rich diversity of school provision – private, public, denominational, secular[38] – but the diversity has broadened considerably over the last decade as new providers of education, including Academy chains, not-for-profit education providers and now free school providers respond to the challenges of urban education. The long-term consequences of school autonomy envisage schools taking increasing control of the full range of their operations. That autonomy, already well-established in relation to staffing and budgets, is being extended, albeit in a managed market, to curriculum, estates and strategic development of schools. However, as schools and school chains become increasingly assured of their ability to manage their own development, the danger is that they think solely of their own interests, and particularly so at a time when government spending is constrained. The international evidence on the effectiveness of diversity of school supply is mixed at best, but there is no reliable evidence that changing governance structures alone will improve outcomes.[39]

Scenarios	Summary of characteristics
Bureaucratic school systems	Powerful bureaucratic systems, resistance to radical change. Schools knitted together into national systems in complex administrative arrangements.
	Political and media commentaries are frequently critical in tone; despite the criticisms, radical change is resisted.
	No major increase in overall funding. Further extension of schools' duties further stretches resources.
	The use of ICT continues to grow without changing schools' main organisational structures.
	A distinct teacher corps persists; strong unions/associations but problematic professional status and rewards.
Widening disparities	A major crisis of teacher shortages, highly resistant to conventional policy responses. Crisis triggered by a rapidly ageing profession, exacerbated by low teacher morale and buoyant opportunities in more attractive graduate jobs.
	The large size of the teaching force means long lead times before policy measures show tangible results on overall teacher numbers.
	Wide disparities in the depth of the crisis by socio-geographic, as well as subject, area.
	Different pathways in response to 'meltdown' – a vicious circle of retrenchment and conflict or emergency strategies spur innovation and change.

contd.

Scenarios	Summary of characteristics
Schools as learning organisations	Schools revitalised around a strong knowledge rather than social agenda, in a culture of high quality, experimentation, diversity and innovation.
	Flourishing new forms of evaluation and competence assessment.
	Large majority of schools justify the label 'learning organisations' – strong knowledge management and extensive links to tertiary education.
	Substantial investments, especially in disadvantaged communities, to develop flexible, state-of-the-art facilities. ICT used extensively.
	Equality of opportunity is the norm and not in conflict with 'quality' agenda.
Schools as social centres	Schools enjoy widespread recognition as the most effective bulwark against social and family fragmentation. Strongly defined by community tasks
	Extensive shared responsibilities between schools and other community bodies, sources of expertise and tertiary education.
	A wide range of organisational forms and settings, with strong emphasis on non-formal learning.
	Generous levels of financial support – to ensure quality learning environments in all communities and high esteem for teachers and schools.
	ICT used extensively, especially for communication and networking.
	A core of high-status teaching professionals, with varied arrangements and conditions but good rewards for all – many others around the core.

contd.

Scenarios	Summary of characteristics
Radical extension of the market	Many new providers in the learning market, with radical reforms of funding, incentives and regulation. Diversity of provision but schools survive.
	Key role of choice – of those buying educational services and of those, such as employers, giving market value to different learning routes. Strong focus on cognitive outcomes but also possibly of values.
	Indicators and accreditation arrangements displace direct public monitoring and curriculum regulation.
	Innovation abounds as do painful transitions and inequalities.
	New learning professionals – public, private; full-time, part-time – are created in the learning markets.
Learning networks	Networks based on diverse parental, cultural, religious and community interests – some local, others using distance and cross-border networking.
	Small group, home schooling and individualised arrangements become widespread. Reduction of existing patterns of governance and accountability.
	Exploitation of powerful, inexpensive ICT.
	Specific professionals called 'teachers' disappear. Demarcations – between teacher and student, parent and teacher, education and community – blur and break down. New learning professionals emerge.

Figure 3: OECD 'ideal type' scenarios for 2020

The ultimate challenge of school autonomy is the challenge it poses for social equity. The evidence base on whether extending parental choice has produced greater social differentiation between schools is deeply contested,[40] but the interaction between school structures and educational outcomes is widely acknowledged.[41] It is notable that much of the international evidence on the value of school autonomy to school improvement is based on more restrictive autonomy than is already the norm in England. Nevertheless, there is evidence that the balance between substantial school autonomy and school support can be managed effectively, not least from the OFSTED evaluation of London Challenge. London Challenge was an extended programme of support to schools, normally provided by schools, albeit driven by external pressure and support. School improvement partnership boards provided the external framework for a school causing concern, ensured an accurate audit of needs and brokered the resources necessary to meet those needs. Its impact was stunning: between 2003 when the programme was established and 2010 when the programme ended, secondary schools in London improved at a faster rate and performed better than schools in the rest of England in terms of their examination results; London primary schools improved faster than those in the rest of England. There are two key messages from London Challenge: the first is that improvement can be driven in a largely devolved education system by schools themselves only when externally supported and challenged; and the second is that such improvement depends on a shared moral imperative that what matters for school leaders is not simply their own school but the needs of learners in other schools.[42]

The practices and behaviours of teachers: improving the quality of teaching

I have discussed the performance of our education system and the organisation of our schools; what of teachers themselves? It has become a principal tenet of education reform that 'nothing is more important than the quality of teaching',[43] and this is perhaps where policy borrowing has been most marked. Michael Barber, formerly a professor at the IOE and subsequently head of standards and effectiveness and head of the prime minister's delivery unit, and then global education partner for McKinsey's, put it in a now famous aphorism: 'the quality of a country's education system cannot exceed the quality of its teachers'.[44] The research findings are striking: Slater, Davies and Burgess conclude that 'having a very effective, rather than an average teacher raises each pupil's attainment by a third of a GCSE grade (0.1–0.25 standard deviations)'.[45] In their recent review of the research on teacher quality for the Sutton Trust, Murphy and Machin return us to the PISA rankings. They state:

> *Bringing the lowest-performing 5–10 per cent of teachers in the UK up to the average would greatly boost attainment and lead to a sharp improvement in the UK's international ranking. All other things equal, in 5 years the UK's rank among OECD countries would improve from 21st in Reading to as high as 7th, and from 22nd in Maths to as high as 12th (0.22 Standard Deviations); over 10 years (the period a child is in the UK school system before the PISA examinations) [sic] the UK would improve its position to as high as 3rd in Reading, and as high as 5th in Maths (0.41 Standard Deviations).[46]*

It is worth taking a moment to consider the evidence. First, there is a circularity to the argument: better teachers are those whose students achieve better, so that those students who achieved better must have been taught by better teachers. In practice, this does not necessarily provide a basis for identifying in advance which teachers are likely to produce better outcomes. Second, other factors still matter. Fenton Whelan, often quoted (albeit selectively) by ministers around the world alongside Michael Barber's studies of high-performing school systems, provides a useful summary:

> *School systems need to ensure that their curricula are relevant and contain enough flexibility to accommodate different learners and different social and economic needs. They need to ensure that school buildings are in good condition...All these things are important and ultimately [have an] impact [on] academic performance. However, none is nearly as important as the quality of teaching* [emphasis added].[47]

Third, there is a frequent slip in the wording of research findings, one that fails to recognise that it is teach*ing* quality which matters rather more than teach*er* quality. In this respect, Michael Barber's aphorism is wrong: it is the quality of teaching, not the quality of teachers, which matters most. The latter, of course, is something policy-makers can be seen to act on far more easily than the former – not least through drives to attract the best graduates to teaching.

There is some evidence, for example from the experience of *Teach First* and *Teach for America*, that attracting highly-committed, well-qualified and well-trained new teachers to schools which are facing serious staffing challenges can make a significant short-term difference to pupil outcomes. It is not clear, however, if the critical difference is made by the trainees' academic qualifications, the mission-driven nature of the programme, the relatively long training, or the staffing boost to otherwise often struggling schools. We should also remember that as a solution to the 'quality problem', recruiting better new teachers into the profession is a relatively long-term, slow burn one. As Dylan Wiliam has pointed out:

> if we were able to raise the threshold for entry into teaching so that we no longer recruited the least effective 10 per cent of teachers, this would take 20 to 30 years to work through the system, and would increase average teacher quality by around 0.2 standard deviations.[48]

The deeper problem, though, is that we still have only a poor sense of which teacher qualities are strongly correlated with excellent classroom performance over time,[49] and there is some evidence to suggest that teachers are differentially effective with different groups of pupils.[50] It is much easier to assert the importance of really outstanding teaching – we all know it when we see it – than it is to understand what it is we need to do to get more of it.

We must stick with this, though, because there are so many blind allies in trying to improve pupil outcomes. The perennial debate over class size provides an example. The largest study of class size reduction remains the 1989 Student Teacher Achievement Ratio (STAR) project in Tennessee, for which approximately 10,000 children were randomly assigned to one of three classes: a class of approximately 15, a class of approximately 23 or a large class with a teaching assistant. Overall, pupils in smaller classes performed more strongly than peers in larger classes – teaching assistants made no difference. However, after four years in smaller classes, the learning gain was the equivalent of around just two months of schooling: in other words, as Eric Hanushek points out, while reducing class size from 23 to 15 would imply employing 50 per cent more teachers, the gain would only be about the same effect as extending the school year by about 10 days.[51]

Just why was the reduction in class size so ineffective? Admittedly, the basis for comparison underpinning the intervention was quite narrow – the difference between a class size of 15 and a class size of 23 is relatively small. More importantly, though, the STAR project failed to control for the quality or length of teaching experience of teachers employed. It may be that teaching quality was weaker in the smaller classes if, as Peter Blatchford suggests, teaching in larger classes requires the deployment of more complex classroom management skills. Hanushek concludes, 'the ultimate effect of any large-scale programme to reduce class size will depend much more...on the quality of new teachers hired than on the effects of class size reductions per se.'[52] So, the class size issue resolves into a question about teaching practices – about what teachers actually do in classrooms with learners to promote learning and improve outcomes.

For some commentators, the debate about classroom teaching is simply outdated: teaching practices are themselves on the verge of transformation by digital technologies – although, as Diana Laurillard pointed out in her inaugural lecture at the Institute, they have been on this verge for some considerable time.[53] As the OECD study on future scenarios hinted, digital technologies offer the potential of transformational change in teaching and learning,[54] dissolving the boundaries of the classroom by making vast information archives accessible to all, shifting the role of the teacher from a provider of information to an adviser and coach, and raising questions about the classroom and the school as a physical entity given that they enable learning to take place – as the Martini ad once had it – 'any time, any place, anywhere'.[55] These are profound challenges to assumptions about teaching and learning. However – and the point at which these two apparently disconnected debates about class size and digital technologies intersect – the position is more complex and once again depends on the teacher. As Diana Laurillard pointed out, information technologies which have been most enthusiastically adopted by teachers in schools and universities are those which are attentional and which by and large reinforce conventional pedagogies.[56] Carey Jewitt and Gemma Moss, evaluating the impact of interactive whiteboards in London schools discovered that the deployment of this technology led to a greater emphasis on the presentation of material *to* pupils[57] (Figure 4).

Figure 4: Henry of Germany discovers the interactive whiteboard (with thanks to Dan Sinclair)

There is an extensive literature on the influences on teacher behaviours[58] which suggests that they are rooted in relationships between tradition, cultural norms, institutional norms and practices and individual motivations. Neither structural changes such as class size reduction, nor technological changes, nor drives to improve the quality of recruits are in and of themselves levers for changing and improving teaching and learning. Worst of all is the assumption that there are silver bullets in the form of faddish innovations, be they, for example, ideas about multiple intelligences[59] or learning styles,[60] or shifting approaches to the teaching of early reading.[61] Improving teaching – transforming teaching – is hard work and depends on understanding what good teachers do to improve outcomes.[62] It involves unlocking the relationship between what teachers know and what they do.[63] Fundamentally, it involves building the teachers' repertoire through developing their knowledge of successful practices, building their skills in analysing evidence from pupils, and their ability to make interventions in pupil learning based on using this evidence. The most successful strategies and programmes involve drawing together a clear understanding of what outstanding practice looks like based on effective research on teacher learning and behaviour change, coupled with sustained support for change in practice through peer support and coaching and mentoring. Peter Matthews's evaluation of the Outstanding Teacher programme shows how this is already in place in a number of our schools.[64] Teaching is above all a social activity: improving teaching involves change in what schools do as organisations as much as what individual teachers do.

Aspirations: what is an institute of education for?

The pressures on teaching and learning in the twenty-first century are extensive in range and intensive in impact. The challenges for teachers and schools are considerable. So what is an institute of education for? One response to this question is implied in the structure and presentation of my argument so far. Throughout my analysis, I have drawn extensively, and deliberately, on the work of colleagues here at the Institute, and, by implication I have demonstrated the fundamental role of higher education as an analyst, documenter and commentator on the development of policy and practice. Above all else, universities are concerned with **knowledge creation**, through what Lawrence Stenhouse called 'systematic sustained enquiry'.[65] One of the powerful things we have learnt through the work of colleagues across this Institute is the importance of locating understandings of teaching and learning in the wider context of social science practices, exploring the ways in which educational practices themselves are changed by social practices just as they seek to change them. For example, children use technology in schools, but they are also, increasingly, digital technology users in their own right and we will not understand the one except in the context of the other: learners' lives beyond schools shape their learning in schools. The task of knowledge creation is fundamental to the work of a university and an institute of education in particular, simply because of the power which comes from being able to make connections between the questions which practitioners, policy-makers and academics ask. Knowledge creation goes far, far beyond the development of successful practices: it needs to pose challengingly critical questions about purpose, function, setting and context, and it needs to relate education to social science more generally. If we are genuinely to build success in education systems, however, we need to ensure that the complexity of schools and schooling, of teachers and teaching and of learners and learning is built into system knowledge.

The second principal function of an institute of education is what is increasingly called **knowledge mobilisation**. Sidney Webb's aspirations for the London Day Training College were clear – and quite right – on this matter: his understanding of the role of the university was couched strongly in terms of the application of learning to improving lives. Fast-forward 100 years and we have Lee Shulman's famous call in the mid-1980s for a knowledge base for teaching as a foundation for long-term teacher improvement. Hiebert has more recently set out to map such a knowledge base,[66] and the research base for successful teaching has expanded enormously. That research base has been extended in particular through synthesis methodologies, especially John Hattie's exhaustive meta-analysis of 50,000 studies of the impact of internal and external factors on learning outcomes,[67] and David Gough's development of synthesis methodologies in the EPPI-Centre at the Institute.[68] As a result, we understand, for example, the powerful impact of feedback on learning outcomes, of peer learning, of secure behaviour management. Equally, we understand the relative unimportance of, for example, setting and streaming, summer schools and team teaching.[69] These are triumphs of knowledge creation which go far beyond Adams's prescription of the knowledge base of teaching in 1902. A critical role for an institute of education is ensuring that its activities –

in all its teaching and all its consultancy – are built from the research and knowledge base, and that this knowledge base is placed at the disposal of practitioners. Knowledge mobilisation increasingly involves being imaginative about dissemination and communication routes: blogs and social networking as well as lectures, seminars and papers.

Yet the gap between what we know and what we deploy in practice remains. Conventionally, the challenge to knowledge mobilisation is seen in either *supply* or *demand* terms. As a supply problem, the issue would disappear if only university researchers found ways of communicating their findings differently.[70] In line with this assessment, significant effort has been invested by research funders in developing programmes to support dissemination and impact. As a demand problem, it is argued, the problem would disappear if only practitioners and policy-makers played a greater role in research commissioning,[71] or we organised differently to develop what David Hargreaves, writing about schools, calls 'knowledge-creating schools'.[72] In fact, as Ben Levin and Judy Sebba have argued, the problem is more complex than that: the pressures, contexts and incentives on researchers, on practitioners and on policy-makers all conspire against effective mobilisation so – to quote Ben Levin again – 'the effort to link them has to be a very deliberate effort that takes into account those different worlds'.[73] The demands are considerable, and in an education system which is increasingly devolved, increasingly autonomous, increasingly diverse, they are likely to become greater without 'deliberate effort'. Yet that effort is acutely needed. Teaching in the twenty-first century, for all the continuities which underpinned the classrooms we looked at and the structures we explored, needs a series of shifts if it is to meet the challenges facing learners.[74] Classrooms are more diverse, schools more complex and the pressures on school systems more profound than they have been. If teaching lies at the heart of this, then teaching needs to be evidence-informed, innovation-oriented and open-minded.

The task of improving practices to improve outcomes and equity is hard, often forbidding work. It meets barriers within institutions and barriers because of the pressures – political, economic, social – to which institutions are subject. Building knowledge and mobilising it for change depend on something more, and I shall describe that as **knowledge engagement** – a profound, open engagement with practices and institutions and a willingness to test the processes of knowledge creation and mobilisation in that engagement; a willingness to work collaboratively at each stage of the process of problem identification, knowledge creation and knowledge mobilisation; and, above all, a willingness to grasp the moral imperative of improvement for all. Practice-based learning is the dominant mode of professional learning, inter-relationships between knowledge and skill are increasingly clear, and institutions themselves are more fluid entities. In this context, knowledge mobilisation depends on being involved.

At various times over the past century, the Institute has been a training college, a centre for curriculum development, a centre for in-service training, a research powerhouse; in the education world of the twenty-first century it does indeed need to be many of these things, but it needs to be them through a more open and fluid relationship with practice and practitioners, with policy and policy-makers, and with those whom they serve. It needs to develop institutional forms which allow for these relationships to become more firmly embedded. As I said at the outset of this lecture, I will betray my own concerns. I want to focus therefore on knowledge creation, mobilisation and engagement in the relationship between schools and universities in supporting teacher development, and to ask whether the structures exist to maximise the relationships. Other professions do have the structures that support knowledge mobilisation and engagement, most notably the medical profession, mediated through deaneries. A deanery works across medical institutions and clusters of institutions to plan, organise and develop medical education. It is a regional structure which brings together the key players in a common framework geared around developing and supporting practitioners by ensuring that development at all stages is coherent and underpinned by research. It is simultaneously not an institution – because it draws together other institutions – and an institution – because it operates as an organisational entity.

It may be that such a framework provides one model for thinking about the relationship between schools, colleges and an institute of education. My argument in this lecture is that teaching and learning in the twenty-first century face immense challenges and that mobilising responses to those challenges depends on drawing together an understanding of the range and inter-relationship of the challenges, the knowledge base for successful teaching and a framework for relating the two. We have been better at the first two of these than the third. If we are to succeed, we need also to explore the third: the shifting relationship between knowledge creation and knowledge deployment. We need the confidence, imagination and ambition to create structures which will allow us genuinely to transform education for all by drawing together what we know and what we might do. Those structures need to be much more deeply embedded than either current consultative or partnership working or models based on commercially trading services can be. They should involve arrangements which reflect the complexity of the relationship between knowledge creation and knowledge mobilisation, and see it as a collective activity in an organisational setting.[75] They should involve commitment to building knowledge about practice at the same time as improving practice. They should place an institute of education at the heart of the transformations which practice is experiencing, locally, nationally and globally, and in mediating the relationships between them. We need the courage and commitment to do this in settings where the barriers to improvement are most entrenched.

Destinations: the Institute, London and the world of education

The Institute of Education was established at what was thought to be a time of extensive change in society, at a time when the long-term consequences of industrialisation, imperialism and the emergence of a class society were becoming increasingly apparent. There are those who might argue that this Institute of Education has responded to – and contributed to – almost continuous change since its foundation in 1902. The educational world of the twenty-first century faces change on a more profound scale, global in scope and local in effect. Structures, practices and pedagogy are all shifting. It is simultaneously a destabilising and an exhilarating time. London remains a compelling educational laboratory, as teachers and learners respond to its variety: immense wealth and appalling poverty side by side; linguistic diversity; challenges for economic change and social cohesion; drivers for excellence, equity and sustainability deeply intertwined. The Institute's claims as a world-leading centre are deeply embedded in the interactions which learning, teaching and living in London involve.

All universities themselves change and develop, and, broadly speaking, they are now subject to similar pressures the world over. Carnegie Mellon University was founded at roughly the same time as the Institute and has followed a similar trajectory: founded as a trade school, it became an institute of technology and now a world leading research centre, always, like the Institute, asking itself questions about its purpose. In 2008, Carnegie Mellon reviewed its strategic plan. The new plan begins like this:

We measure excellence by the impact we have on making the world better...Building on deeply grounded research strength, we collaborate across disciplines and the initiative to do so comes from the ground up, not the top down...We view teaching and research to be on the same continuum of knowledge creation, so that all have the chance to develop deep knowledge...and to grasp how new ideas can change the world.[76]

'We measure excellence by the impact we have on making the world better.' This is a time of profound, destabilising change in education. The pressures are intense. Learning and teaching are in an uneasy relationship with the demands of the economy and profound shifts in society and technology. If the Institute was established in a society where the routines of classrooms were governed by the needs of the industrial economy, what sort of learning enterprises are needed for the kinds of society and social practices which are emerging?

The challenge of teaching and learning today calls for a re-alignment of the relationship between this Institute and the academic, policy, practitioner communities it serves. The globalisation of policy, the shift towards autonomous schools and networks, the development of a strong research and evidence base for teaching, and the deployment of digital technologies, pose tough questions. More than ever, the role of an institute of education is not just to develop answers, but, through its own close engagement with policy, practice and user communities, to shape practices. The task of an institute of education is to marshal its own academic resources, and the resources of its partners, in an intellectual and practical project: re-visioning schooling, re-visioning teaching and re-visioning learning for the twenty-first century through the engagements we promote.

Acknowledgements

I am extremely grateful to Andy Buck, Ben Levin, Sandy Leaton Gray, Martin Roberts, and, especially, Emma Wisby, for their thoughtful comments on early and developing versions of this lecture. Emma in particular has been invaluable in examining drafts, detecting flaws in the argument and identifying supporting material. The errors and mistakes remain, of course, my own.

Notes

1   Aldrich, R. (2002) *The Institute of Education, 1902–2002: A centenary history*. London: Institute of Education, University of London, p. 5.

2   Gordon, P. (ed.) (1900) *The Study of Education: A collection of inaugural lectures. Vol I. Early and modern*. London: Woburn Press, p. 48.

3   Aldrich (2002), p. 9.

4   Brennan, E.J.T. (ed.) (1975) *Education for National Efficiency: The contribution of Sidney and Beatrice Webb*. London: Athlone Press, pp. 143–7, quoted in Aldrich (2002), p. 9.

5   Ives, E. (2000) *The First Civic University: Birmingham, 1880–1980. An Introductory History*. Birmingham: University of Birmingham Press, pp. 40–2. Cambridge University introduced a certificate examination in education in 1880 and Oxford in 1897: Searby, P. (1982) *The Training of Teachers in Cambridge University: The first sixty years, 1879–1939*. Cambridge: Cambridge University Press, pp. 1, 10; Honey, J.R. De S. and Curthoys, M.C. (2000) 'Oxford and schooling', in M.G. Brock and M.C. Curthoys (eds), *The History of the University of Oxford. Vol VII: Nineteenth century Oxford, Part 2*. Oxford: Oxford University Press, pp. 556–7.

6   McKibbin, R. (1998) *Classes and Cultures: England 1918–1951*. Oxford: Oxford University Press, pp. 206–8; Harrison, J.F.C. (1990) *Late Victorian Britain, 1875–1901*. London: Fontana, pp. 203, 205; Broadberry, S. (2004) 'Human capital and skills', in R. Floud and P. Johnson (eds), *The Cambridge Economic History of Modern Britain. Vol II: Economic maturity, 1860–1939*. Cambridge: Cambridge University Press, pp. 58–9.

7   Aldrich (2002), p. 87.

8   For example, HESA data for 2009/10 puts the IOE in the top three institutions for social science research income. See <www.hesa.ac.uk> (accessed 29 November 2011).

9   Laurentius de Voltolina: *Liber ethicorum des Henricus de Alemannia;* Kupferstichkabinett SMPK. Berlin: Berlin/Staatliche Museen Preussischer Kulturbesitz, Min. 1233.

10   From Towlson, C.W. (ed) *Woodhouse Grove School, 1812-1962*. Reprinted with permission from Woodhouse Grove School. I am grateful to the Institute archivist, Sarah Aitchison, for sourcing this photograph.

11   See <www.campaign-for-learning.org.uk/projects/L2L/The%20Project/Project.htm> (accessed 30 November 2011).

12   Riley, K.A. (2010) *Are London's Schools Meeting the Needs of Today's Young People?* London: Institute of Education, University of London.

13   Fraser, G. (2011) 'Thought for the Day', *Today* programme, BBC Radio 4, 5 November.

14   Block, D. (2006) *Multilingual Identities in a Global City: London stories*. London: Palgrave.

15   For example, see Dorling, D. (2011) *Fair Play: A Daniel Dorling reader in social justice*. Bristol: Policy Press, pp. 65–83; Brewer, M., Sibieta, L. and Wren-Lewis, L. (2010) *Racing Away: Income inequality and the evolution of high incomes*. London: Institute of Fiscal Studies, Briefing Note 76.

16   White, J. (2001) *London in the Twentieth Century: A city and its people*. London: Viking, pp. 161–2, 360–2, 380–3; McKibbin, R. (1998) *Classes and Cultures*; Rosen, A. (2003) *The*

Transformation of British Life, 1950–2000: A social history. Manchester: Manchester University Press, pp. 81–3; on the raising of the participation age to 18 see <www.education.gov. uk/16to19/participation/rpa> (accessed 2 November 2011).

17   Lubienski, C. (2010) *The Charter School Experiment: Expectations, evidence, and implications*. Cambridge, MA: Harvard Educational Press; Brouilette, L. (2002) *Charter Schools: Lessons in school reform*. Mahwah, NJ: Lawrence Erlbaum Associates.

18   Gunter, H. (2011) *The State and Education Policy: The Academies programme*. London: Continuum.

19   Kopp, W. (2011) *A Chance To Make History: What works and what doesn't in providing an excellent education for all*. New York: Public Affairs; Ness, M. (2004) *Lessons to Learn: Voices from the front lines of Teach for America*. London and New York: RoutledgeFalmer; <www. teachforall.org/network_locations.html> (accessed 21 October 2011).

20   See: on UTCS, <www.utcolleges.org/> (accessed 28 October 2011); for the establishment of the first Korean meister schools, <www.koreatimes.co.kr/www/news/ nation/2011/04/116_61696.html> (accessed 28 October 2011).

21   Levin, B. (2010) 'The challenge of large scale literacy reform'. *School Effectiveness and School Improvement*, 21(4), 359–76.

22   Sorkin, A.R. (2009) *Too Big to Fail: Inside the battle to save Wall Street*. London and New York: Allen Lane.

23   Chowdry, H. and Sibieta, L. (2011) 'Trends in Education and Schools Spending'. *Institute for Fiscal Studies (IFS) Briefing Note BN121*. London: Institute for Fiscal Studies.

24   For example, Archer, M.S. (1979) *Social Origins of Educational Systems*. London and Beverly Hills: Sage.

25   Autor, D.H., Levy, F. and Murnane, R.J. (2003) 'The skill content of recent technological change: an empirical exploration'. *Quarterly Journal of Economics*, 1184 (November), 1279–334; Levy, F. and Murnane, R. (2004) *The New Division of Labor: How computers are creating the new job market*. Princeton, NJ: Princeton University Press and Russell Sage Foundation.

26   Department for Education (DfE) (2011) *GCSE and Equivalent Results in England. 2010/11 Provisional: 20th October*; <www.education.gov.uk/rsgateway/DB/SFR/s001034/index. shtml> (accessed 1 November 2011): 58.3 per cent achieved 5 or more GCSEs at grade A* to C or equivalent including English and mathematics GCSEs; 59.0 per cent achieved English and mathematics GCSEs at grades A* to C; 78.8 per cent achieved 5 or more GCSEs at grade A* to C or equivalent.

27   Isaacs, T. (forthcoming) 'The role of international assessment in improving education quality, with special emphasis on the UAE', in *Proceedings of the ECSSR's Second Annual Education Conference*, Abu Dhabi: ECSSR, p. 12; Hopmann, S.T. and Brinek, G. (2007) 'PISA according to PISA: does PISA keep what it promises?', in S.T. Hopmann, G. Brinek and M. Tetzl (eds) *PISA zufolge PISA/PISA According to PISA*. Berlin and Vienna: LIT Verlag, pp. 9–19.

28   Organisation for Economic Co-operation and Development (OECD) (2010) *PISA 2009 Results: What students can do in English, Mathematics and Science. Vol 1*. Paris: OECD.

29   Harris, A. (2009) *Equity and Diversity: Building community. Improving schools in challenging circumstances*. London: Institute of Education, University of London.

30   Kelly, A.V. (2004) *The Curriculum: Theory and practice*, 5th edition. London: Sage.

31   For example, see Bassett, D. (2011) *Times Educational Supplement*, 18 February; and, for a counterview, <http://abetterbaccalaureate.org/> (accessed 29 November 2011).

32   Schwartz, R. (2011) *Pathways to Prosperity: Meeting the challenges of preparing young Americans for the twenty-first century*. Cambridge, MA: Harvard, Graduate School of Education.

33   Young, M.F.D. (2007) *Bringing Knowledge Back In: From social constructivism to social realism in the sociology of education*. London: Routledge.

34   Layard, R. (2007) 'Happiness and the teaching of values'. *Centrepiece* 12(1),18–23.

35   James, L., Guile, D. and Unwin, L. (2011) *From Learning for the Knowledge-Based Economy to Learning for Growth: Re-examining clusters, innovation and qualifications*. London: IOE, Centre for Learning and Life Chances in Knowledge Economies and Societies; <www.llakes.org> (accessed 29 November 2011).

36   Organisation for Economic Co-operation and Development (OECD) (2006) *Schooling for Tomorrow: Think scenarios, rethink education*. Paris: OECD; Organisation for Economic Co-operation and Development (OECD) (2006) *Demand-Sensitive Schooling? Evidence and issues*. Paris: OECD; Organisation for Economic Co-operation and Development (OECD) (2001) *Education Policy Analysis 2001*. Paris: OECD; and see <www.oecd.org/dataoecd/56/39/38967594.pdf> (accessed 28 October 2011).

37   Gunter (2011) *The State and Education Policy*; Department for Education (2010) *The Importance of Teaching: Schools White Paper*. London: Department for Education.

38   McClure, S. (1970) *A History of Education in London, 1870–1970*. London: Allen Lane; Brighouse, T. and Fullick, L. (eds) (2007) *Education in a Global City: Essays from London*. London: Institute of Education, University of London.

39   Centre for Research on Education Outcomes (CREDO) (2009) *Multiple Choice: Charter schools in 16 states*. Stanford, CA: CREDO.

40   Gorard, S. (2009) 'Does the index of segregation matter? The composition of secondary schools in England since 1996'. *British Educational Research Journal*, 35(4), 639–52.

41   Allen, R. and Vignoles, A. (2007) 'Market incentives in schools', in F. Coffield and R. Steer (eds), *Public Sector Reform: Principles for improving the education system*. London: Institute of Education, University of London; see also, European Group for Research on Equity in Education Systems (EGREES) (2008) *Developing a Sense of Justice Among Disadvantaged Students: The role of schools*. Birmingham: EGREES; Gorard, S., Taylor, C. and Fitz, J. (2003) *Schools, Markets and Choice Policies*. London: RoutledgeFalmer.

42   OFSTED (2010) *London Challenge*, London: OFSTED.

43   Barber, M. and Mourshed, M. (2007) *How the World's Best Education Systems Come out on Top*. London and New York: McKinsey, p. 7; Whelan, F. (2009) *Lessons Learned: How good policies produce better schools*. London: Fenton Whelan, pp. 33–5, 117–124; Hanushek, E. (2011) 'The Economic Value of Higher Teacher Quality'. *Economics of Education Review* 30(3), 466–79; Department for Education (2010) *The Importance of Teaching*. London: Department for Education; and see <www.pearsonfoundation.org/oecd/> (accessed 29 October 2011).

44 Barber and Mourshed (2007), p. 5.

45 Slater, H., Davies, N. and Burgess, S. (2009) 'Do teachers matter? Measuring the variation in teacher effectiveness in England'. *CMPO Working Paper* 09/212; see also Rivkin, S.G., Hanushek, E.F. and Kain, J.F. (2005) 'Teachers, schools and academic achievement'. *Econometrica*, 732, 417–45.

46 Machin, S. and Murphy, S. (2011) *Improving the Impact of Teachers on Pupil Achievement in the UK: Interim findings*. London: Sutton Trust, p. 5.

47 Whelan (2009), p. 33.

48 Wiliam, D. (2009) 'Teacher quality: the crucial ingredient of high-performing education systems', unpublished paper; Jepsen, C. and Rivkin, S.G. (2002) 'What is the Trade-off between Smaller Classes and Teacher Quality?'. *Vol. 9205*. Cambridge, MA: National Bureau of Economic Research.

49 Hanushek, E. and Welch, F. with Rivkin, S. (2006) 'Teacher Quality', in E.A. Hanushek and F. Welch (eds) *Handbook of the Economics of Education. 2: North-Holland*. Amsterdam: Elsevier; see also, Gladwell, M. (2008) 'Most likely to succeed: How do we hire when we can't tell who's right for the job?'. *New Yorker*, December 15; <www.newyorker.com/reporting/2008/12/15/081215fa_fact_gladwell#ixzz1clg7nPuq> (accessed 28 October 2011).

50 Slater, H., Davies, N. and Burgess, S. (2009) 'Do teachers matter? Measuring the variation in teacher effectiveness in England'. *Centre for Market and Public Organisation (CMPO) Working Paper* 09/212, Bristol: CMPO, p. 11.

51 Hanushek, E.A. (1999) 'Some findings from an independent investigation of the Tennessee STAR experiment and from other investigations of class size effects'. *Educational Evaluation and Policy Analysis*, 21(2), 145–63.

52 Hanushek (1999), p. 162.

53 Laurillard, D. (2008) *Digital technologies and their role in achieving our ambitions for education*. London: Institute of Education, University of London, p. 1.

54 OECD (2006), p. 5.

55 Reynolds, D., Treharne, D. and Tripp, H. (2003) 'ICT: the hopes and the reality'. *British Journal of Educational Technology*, 34(3), 151–67; Somekh, B. (2007) *Pedagogy and Learning with ICT: Researching the art of innovation*. London: Routledge; Pachler, N., Pimmer, C. and Seipold, J. (eds) (2011) *Work-based Mobile Learning: Concepts and cases*. New York: Peter Lang.

56 Laurillard (2008), p. 14.

57 Moss, G., Jewitt , C., Levacic, R., Armstrong, V., Cardini, A. and Castle, F. (2007) *Interactive Whiteboards, Pedagogy, and Pupil Performance: An evaluation of the Schools Whiteboard Expansion Project (London Challenge)*. London: Department for Children, Schools and Families.

58 For example, Ashton, P. and Gregoire-Gill, M. (2003) 'At the heart of teaching: the role of emotion in changing teachers' beliefs', in J. Raths and A.C. McAninch (eds), *Teacher Beliefs and Classroom Performance: The impact of teacher education*. Greenwich, CT: Information Age Publishing, pp. 99–122; Fang, Z. (1996) 'A review of research on teacher beliefs and practices'. *Educational Research*, 38(1), 47–65; Korthagen, F.A.J. and Kessels, J.P.A.M. (1999) 'Linking theory and practice: changing the pedagogy of teacher education'. *Educational*

Researcher 28(4), 4–17; Korthagen, F.A.J., Kessels, J., Koster, B., Lagerwerf, B. and Wubbels, T. (2001) *Linking Practice and Theory: The pedagogy of realistic teacher education*. Mahwah, NJ: Lawrence Erlbaum Associates; Lortie, S. (1975) *Schoolteacher: A sociological study*. Chicago: University of Chicago Press; Richardson, V. and Placier, P. (2001) 'Teacher change', in V. Richardson (ed.), *Handbook of Research on Teaching*, 4th edition. Washington, DC: American Educational Research Association, pp. 905–47; Zeichner, K., Tabachnick, B. and Densmore, K. (1987) 'Individual, institutional and cultural influences on the development of teacher's craft knowledge', in J. Calderhead (ed.), *Exploring Teachers' Thinking*. London: Cassel, pp. 21–59.

59 See White, J. (1998) *Do Howard Gardner's Multiple Intelligences Add Up?*. London: Institute of Education, University of London.

60 Curry, L. (1990) 'One critique of the research on learning styles'. *Educational Leadership*, 48, 50–56; Coffield, F., Moseley, D., Hall, E. and Ecclestone, K. (2004) *Learning Styles and Pedagogy in Post-16 Learning: A systematic and critical review*. London: Learning and Skills Research Centre.

61 For example, see Wyse, D. and Goswami, U. (2008) 'Synthetic phonics and the teaching of reading'. *British Education Research Journal*, 34(6), 691–710.

62 For example, see Siraj-Blatchford, I., Shepherd, D-L., Melhuish, E., Taggart, B., Sammons, P. and Sylva, K. (2011) *Effective Pedagogical Strategies in English and Mathematics in Key Stage 2: A study of Year 5 classroom practices from the EPPSE 3–16 longitudinal study*. London: Department for Education (DfE), RR0129.

63 Leach, J. and Moon, B. (2008) *The Power of Pedagogy*. London: Sage.

64 Matthews, P. (2010) *From Good to Outstanding: Evaluation of the Outstanding Teacher Programme*. London: London Challenge/National College for Leadership in Schools and Children's Services.

65 Stenhouse, L. (1980) *What Counts as Research*? Unpublished mimeo. Norwich: CARE Archive, University of East Anglia.

66 Shulman, L.S. (1987) 'Knowledge and teaching: Foundations of the new reform'. *Harvard Educational Review*, 57(1), 1–22. See also, Hiebert, C., Gallimore, R. and Stigler, J.W. (2003) 'A knowledge base for the teaching profession: What would it look like and how can we get one?'. *Education Researcher*, 31(5), 3–15; Leach and Moon (2008).

67 Hattie, J.W. (2008) *Visible Learning: A synthesis of over 800 meta-analyses relating to achievement*. London: Routledge.

68 Gough, D.A. (2007) 'The evidence for policy and practice information and co-ordinating EPPI Centre', in T. Burns and T. Schuller (eds), *Evidence in Education: Linking research and policy*. Paris: CERI/OECD.

69 Hattie (2008) *Visible Learning*, pp. 77, 89–91, 173–4, 186–7, 219; Black, P.J. and Wiliam, D. (1998) 'Assessment and classroom learning'. *Assessment in Education*, 5(1), 7–74; Black, P.J. and Wiliam, D. (1998) *Inside the Black Box: Raising standards through classroom assessment*. London: King's College; Hattie, J. and Timperley, H. (2007) 'The power of feedback'. *Review of Educational Research*, 77(1), 81–112.

70 Blunkett, D. (2000) *Influence or Irrelevance: Can social science improve government?*. Swindon: ESRC, and Department for Education and Employment; Hargeaves, D. (1996)

'Teaching as a Research Based Profession', *Teacher Training Agency Annual Lecture*. London: Teacher Training Agency.

71 Saunders, L. (2007) *Educational Research Commissioned by/for Policy Audiences*. London: Teaching and Learning Research Programme (TLRP) <www.bera.ac.uk/educational-research-commissioned-byfor-policy-audiences/> (accessed 1 November 2011); Gough, D. (2011) 'User-led reviews of research knowledge: enhancing relevance and reception', in E. Banister *et al.* (eds), *Knowledge Translation in Context: University–community, policy and indigenous approaches*. Toronto: University of Toronto Press.

72 Hargreaves, D. (1999) 'The knowledge creating school'. *British Journal of Educational Studies*, 41(2), 122–44.

73 Interviewed by British Education Research Association (2009); see <www.youtube.com/watch?v=Kkr-xjL8OiQ> (accessed 27 October 2011).

74 International Alliance of Leading Education Institutes (IALEI) (2008) *Transforming 21st Century Teacher Education through Redefined Professionalism, Alternative Pathways and Genuine Partnerships*. Singapore: IALEI.

75 I owe this phrase to Ben Levin, personal communication.

76 Carnegie Mellon (2008) *Strategic Plan*; <www.cmu.edu/strategic-plan/2008-strategic-plan/2008-strategic-plan.pdf > (accessed 29 November 2011).